Bats!

Amazing and Mysterious Creatures of the Night

Marianne Haffner and
Hans-Peter B. Stutz

BLACKBIRCH PRESS, INC.
WOODBRIDGE, CONNECTICUT

The English and Latin names of the bats pictured:

Large mouse-eared bat *(Myotis myotis)*
Common pipistrelle *(Pipistrellus pipistrellus)*
Whiskered bat *(Myotis mystacinus)*
Brown long-eared bat *(Plecotus auritus)*
Noctule bat *(Nyctalus noctula)*
Frosted bat *(Vespertilio murinus)*

Photo Credits
Photos by Hans-Peter B. Stutz
Page 34: Patrick Wiedemeier

Library of Congress Cataloging-in-Publication Data
Haffner, Marianne.
[Fledermäuse die geheimnisvollen Flugakrobaten. English]
Bats! : amazing and mysterious creatures of the night / by Marianne Haffner and Hans-Peter B. Stutz. — 1st ed.
p. cm.
Includes bibliographical references and index.
Summary: Introduces bats by exploring several of the different species, their physical characteristics, behaviors, and habitats.
ISBN 1-56711-214-5 (lib. bdg. : alk. paper)
1. Bats—Juvenile literature. [1. Bats.] I. Stutz, Hans-Peter. II. Title.
QL737.C5H2413 1999
599.4—dc21 97-47100
CIP
AC

Published by Blackbirch Press, Inc.
260 Amity Road
Woodbridge, CT 06525

First Edition

e-mail: staff@blackbirch.com
Web site: www.blackbirch.com

First published in German as *Fledermäuse*.

Printed in Hong Kong

10 9 8 7 6 5 4 3 2 1

Contents

Introduction: Mysterious, but Not Sinister

Most people think bats are scary and mysterious. But few people know the fascinating details about these creatures of the night. In the past, people thought bats did the work of the devil. That's why in much Christian art, demons wear bat wings. In China and Japan, bats have a better reputation. There, they are honored as bringers of good luck.

Bats are not related to mice, nor to birds, even though they fly. They are actually descended from the insectivores (insect-eaters), who include, for example, the hedgehog.

Along with flying foxes—which live in Africa, Asia, and Australia—bats make up their own order in the animal kingdom called the Chiroptera. That word comes from Greek and means "hand-winger." Bats do, in fact, fly by rearranging their hands! They are the only mammals that can actively fly: not with feathered wings, like birds, but with extendable flight membranes. Chiroptera were already living on the earth more than 50 million years ago. With over 900 species, they are the largest order of mammals other than rodents.

Bats can be found in habitats all over the world. More than 25 species can be found in North America alone, and more than 25 species are found in Central Europe.

Most bats feed primarily on insects. Bats have developed a special ability that they use to orient themselves while hunting at night. Through their mouths and noses, they give off ultrasonic (very high frequency) sounds that are produced in the throat. These sounds cannot be heard by human ears. If these tones strike an object—a tree, for example, or an insect—they come back to the bat as an echo. Bats can then perceive and interpret these echoes with their brains. In this way, they get a "sound picture" of their surroundings as they fly. With this sort of "sonar," bats can find their way in the dark and locate their prey.

Today, bats are seriously endangered. Because of real estate development and overuse of land, insect populations have declined in many places. This means bats often lack food. Shelter in old houses and tree hollows is also becoming more and more scarce. This means bats have fewer hiding places in which to rest during the day. For these reasons, bats need the help and cooperation of humans if they are going to survive.

Waking from Winter Sleep

In the spring, when warmer weather hatches mosquito larvae and mosquitoes begin to swarm, bats emerge at dusk from a long winter's sleep.

Above: *Mosquito larvae hatch in the spring, just in time for the hungry bats waking from their winter's sleep.*

Left: *The largest European species of bat—the large mouse-eared bat—weighs 1 ounce (30 grams) and has a wingspan of 16 inches (43 centimeters).*

Having spent the winter hiding away in a deep resting state called hibernation, the bats are hungry. Now they begin to hunt insects through the dark night. Just before dawn, before it is really light, the bats slip back into their hiding places, where they sleep through the day.

Hidden from Daylight

By the time the morning sun comes up over the horizon, all the mouse-eared bats in a colony are already settled in dark hiding places, such as caves or roof rafters. Just before that time, however, there is great noise and confusion while each animal scrambles to find its place. Squeaks and chirps fill the colony as the bats communicate with each other. A few animals hang by themselves. Others hide behind a roof beam. Many hang close together in large clusters. There are so many that one could hardly count them! As soon as the bats settle into their sleeping places, the peeps gradually stop, and peace comes to the colony.

A mouse-eared bat colony can consist of dozens of—or even several hundred—animals.

An Upside-Down Nap

If you looked carefully at a group of mouse-eared bats close up, you would see that these animals don't actually ever fall into a deep sleep. Instead, they look around alertly in their attics or resting places. There is often a lot going on in the colony, especially in the afternoon. If an animal has to release urine or feces, it climbs out of the group or at least turns over so it doesn't dirty itself or its neighbors. Afterwards, however, it has to reclaim its place in the group. This often leads to squeaky high-pitched spats in which the bats clamor loudly!

Above: *Mouse-eared bats don't fall down, even when they're relaxed. A nerve-blocking mechanism in their powerful foot claws allows them to stay securely anchored without the use of muscle power.*

Left: *Adult mouse-eared bats hang very close together, attached to one another. Each animal holds itself up with its feet by clinging to a piece of attached wood or roof beam.*

A Warm Group

Unlike most mammals, a bat's body temperature varies considerably throughout the day. In full activity, such as flight, most bats have a body temperature of almost 104° Fahrenheit (40° Celsius).

During sleep, however, a bat's body temperature adjusts to its surroundings: it is switched to a kind of "energy saver" mode. If it is warm outside, the bats will mainly soak up energy from the sun.

On cool days, a bat's body temperature drops. If a bat is frightened by a human or animal threat, it is completely helpless at first. Before it can move or fly away to escape, it needs a few minutes to warm its body back up to an "active temperature."

Temperature becomes especially important when young bats are being raised. If it is cool for a long time in June, the mother will not find enough insects. If she doesn't have enough to eat, the mother bat will not have enough energy to keep her young warm. Many bat babies die of exhaustion in such years.

Above: *In cooler weather, the bats move close together so they can conserve energy and lose as little body heat as possible.*

Left (opposite): *When they are warm, mouse-eared bats hang in loose groups.*

A Nursery Colony

Male and female bats mate in the fall. During their winter hibernation, the male's sperm remains in "cold storage" in the female's body. Right after the awakening in spring, the sperm become warmed. That is how the female's eggs become fertilized. After a period of about two months—by June—the next generation appears in the nursery colony.

When giving birth, the mother clings to a roof beam with all four feet. She makes a pocket with her tail flight membrane, into which her newborns slide. A mouse-eared bat baby comes into the world feet first and immediately grasps a roof lath. Each female mouse-eared bat delivers a few young. Newborn bats are blind and almost naked.

Opposite: *Mothers cover their young with their wing membranes for protection.*

Top: *Mouse-eared bats do not build nests. The mother simply gives birth to her young while she hangs from the beams!*

Center: *A newborn mouse-eared bat*

Bottom: *A young bat's wings are short and tiny.*

Alone in the Attic

While a mother bat flies off into the night to hunt for insects, her young remain alone. On their first night, bat babies are still totally helpless and will hang, unmoving, in the air. By morning, they are hungry and peep softly. Each one waits anxiously for the return of its mother, who will nurse it right away.

By the second night, the blind young are already crawling around the attic one on top of another. They sniff each other and carefully explore their nursery quarters. As they climb around, they hold on to their supports with their thumb and toe claws.

Bats are very clean animals. For them, keeping clean is an instinct, it is "born" into them. Even young bats lick their wings carefully and thoroughly. Caring for wings is very important to a bat, because wing membranes must never become dried out. For this reason, bats rub special fluids from their facial glands into their wing membranes. This also gives each baby its own scent, which makes it easier for its mother to recognize it by smell.

A baby mouse-eared bat hangs helplessly from the rafters, anxiously awaiting its mother's return.

Personal Care

Young bats grow up quickly. After just a week, they open their eyes and begin using their vision—even though it is poorly adapted to daytime conditions. Throughout the day, the young wake up, stretch, and yawn widely.

Young bats will be nursed by their mothers for about eight weeks. When they are not nursing or sleeping, young bats hang together in "baby groups" and clean themselves from top to bottom. For a "comb," they mainly use their clawed hind feet. They can also stretch

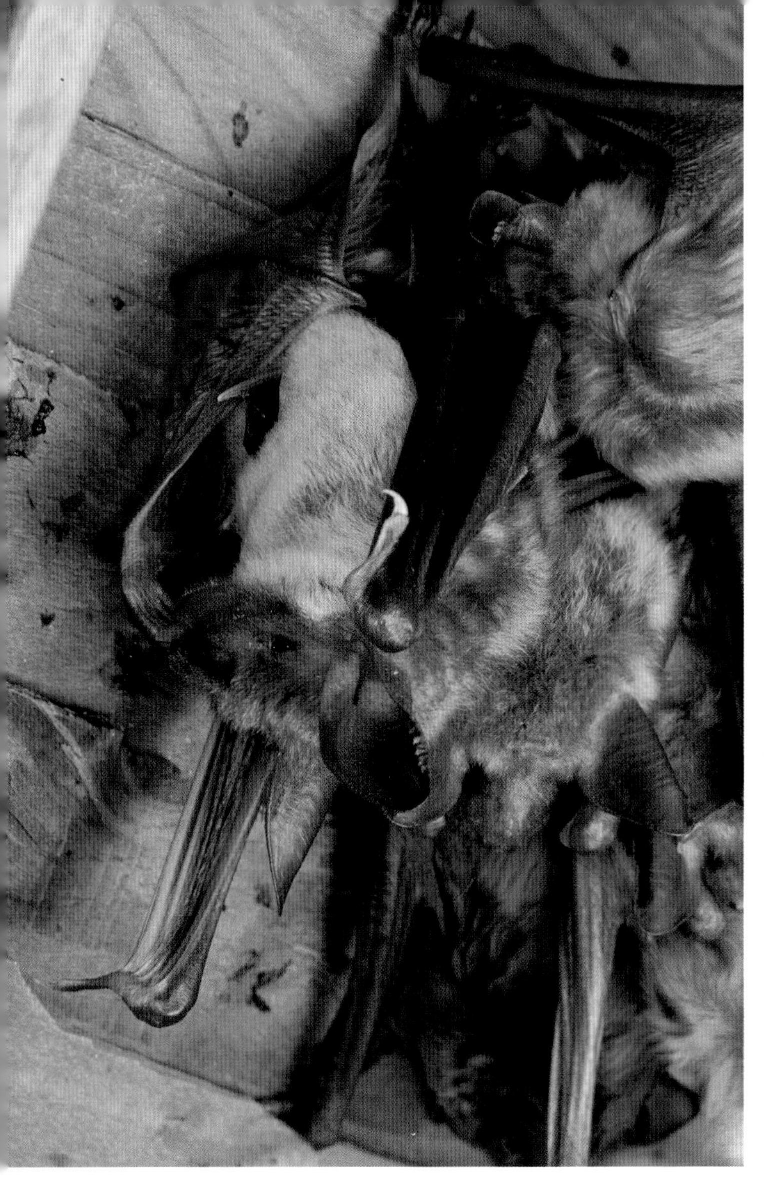

into unbelievable positions and reach every part of their body with their feet to clean themselves.

If the foot "comb" gets dirty, it will be cleaned. To do this, a bat baby puts one foot in its mouth and licks it thoroughly. Then it puts the other foot in. While doing this, it holds on to its anchor beam with only one foot. If it moves a lot or is disturbed by a neighbor, it has to be very careful not to fall down!

Pages 16 and 17: *Young bats hang together as they clean themselves and wait for nursing time.*

Flight School

After six weeks, young bats are almost grown. It is at this time that—during the night—they first try to fly. At first, they can only take short flights straight ahead and onto the next beam. Soon, however, they become more skillful.

Above: *When their mothers return, the young beg loudly for milk.*

Left: *During the night, half-grown mouse-eared bats practice their fluttering flights.*

Within days they are chasing each other around and flitting quickly from beam to beam. Completely exhausted and hungry afterward, they hang from the roof laths again in the early morning and wait for their mothers.

Mouse-eared bats listen to the orienting sounds of other members and can learn the flight path to good hunting areas from each other. Bats will often fly six or more miles (ten or more kilometers) away. They like to follow land-marks such as hedges, brooks in woods, and road borders.

The First Hunt

By the beginning of August, the young bats have grown as large as their mothers. They have also become expert flyers. Now, for the first time, they will leave home in search of food—primarily insects.

Bats have an exceptional place-memory. They know every inch of their hunting area and can navigate with-out constantly using their ultrasound (echolocation) to orient themselves. This skill also comes in handy if they are eating an insect as they fly—it is sometimes difficult for bats to echolocate through a full mouth.

Sparse woods are the preferred hunting grounds of bats. They also find lots of insects over the fields at the edge of a forest.

Many researchers would like to find out exactly where bats hunt for insects in the forest. People have studied mouse-eared bats in laboratories and found the remains of insects still inside. They were almost exclusively rove beetles—beetles that rarely fly. For this reason, it is believed that mouse-eared bats also get their prey from the forest floor and probably even hunt around on the ground like field mice.

Left: *Mouse-eared bats mostly fly low, near the ground. In low flight over the fields at the edge of a forest, they can snap female crane-flies, which lay their eggs in the grass there.*

Below: *Most mouse-eared bats have thick calluses on their feet. It's possible that they hunt rove beetles, such as this one, on foot.*

Left: *A bat's heartbeat and breathing are much slower during hibernation. Body temperature can even reach near freezing point.*

Below: *In certain areas of the world, bat conservationists have constructed special bat doors to ensure an undisturbed hibernation. This is important because each awakening uses up a large amount of the fat reserves that are needed for deep sleep.*

Deep Sleep for Winter

In colder climates, during the fall, bats often have trouble finding enough food. For that reason, they spend the cold time of year in deep hibernation. They fly many miles regularly before they find a suitable burrow.

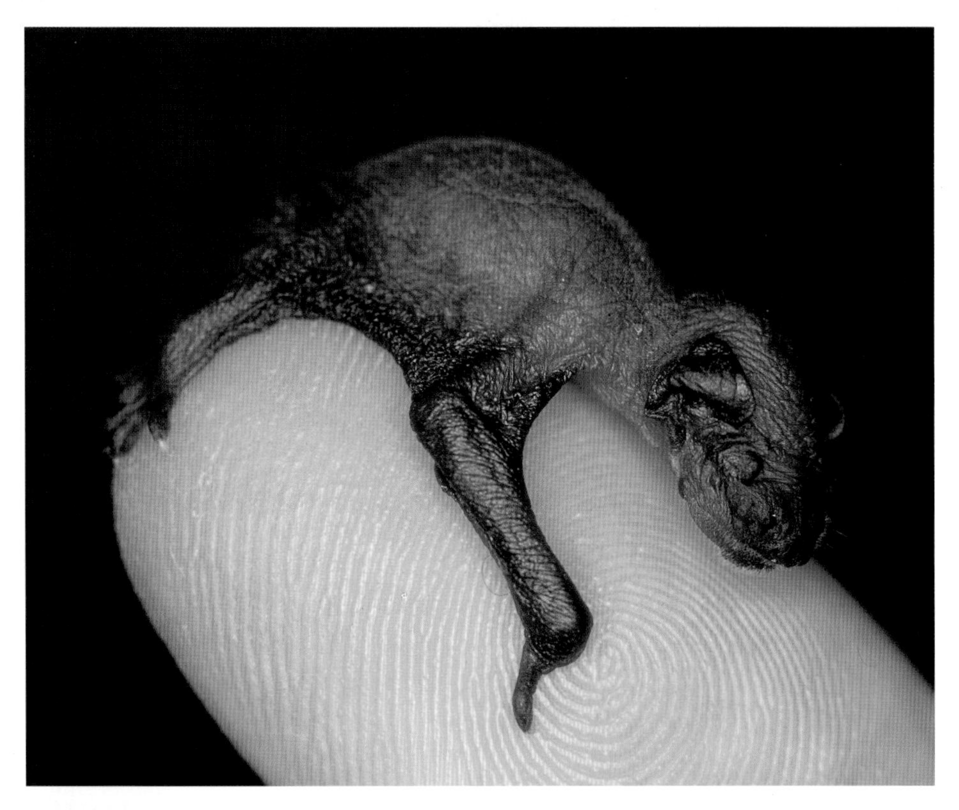

Tiny Hiders

The common pipistrelle is the smallest bat species. It is one of the most abundant species in Europe and is well adapted to surviving in human settlements. Unlike the large litters of other species of bats, pipistrelles frequently give birth to twins. During the day, pipistrelles will often hide in cracks in house exteriors. Crumbs—bat feces that look like mouse droppings—on window sills and balconies are usually the only visible evidence of these little secret lodgers.

Above left: *A newborn pipistrelle is hardly as big as a berry at birth.*

Below left: *Even when grown, pipistrelles are no bigger than an average walnut. Most adults weigh only .2 ounces (6 grams) and have an average wingspan of 8 inches (20 centimeters).*

The common pipistrelle prefers spaces in narrow cracks in walls, behind wall boards, and in roof overhangs.

Whiskered bats will make their homes between the cracks in a wooden barn wall.

Whiskers in Wood

The whiskered bat likes to sleep between the cracks of barn walls during the day. At night, it hunts small flying insects in the tops of fruit trees and in parks.

Like all bat species, the whiskered bat falls into a "stupor" during the day and when it is cool. If it is disturbed, it cannot fly away immediately. In order to sleep safely, it presses itself backward, deep inside the narrowest cracks and crevices it can find.

Above right: *This whiskered bat looks out shyly from its safe hiding place.*

Below right: *When disturbed, it cries out loudly and threatens by baring its pointed teeth.*

A Long-Eared Acrobat

Long-eared bats are true flying acrobats! With their wide wings, they can hover in the air, fluttering in one place for a few moments. Long-eared bats are also skilled at picking off insects—earwigs, caterpillars, and sleeping moths—from leaves and building facades.

Above: *A long-eared bat group hangs in an attic.*

Right: *Wide wings make the long-eared bat an expert acrobat in the air.*

Big ears enable long-eared bats to hear even the softest scratching sounds on the ground below. Such sensitive hearing also allows them to react to any changes in the echoes coming back from their echolocating sounds. When hunting, they can carry large insects, such as moths, to an eating place. There, they bite off the wings—which are not very nutritious—and let them fall to the ground.

Above: *Young long-eared bats have floppy ears just a few days after their birth.*

Opposite page, top left: *When they sleep, long-ears cover their large outer ear with their underarms.*

Opposite page, top right: *When they wake up, they fold their ears out.*

Opposite page, bottom: *Ready to fly away, the ears are fully erect.*

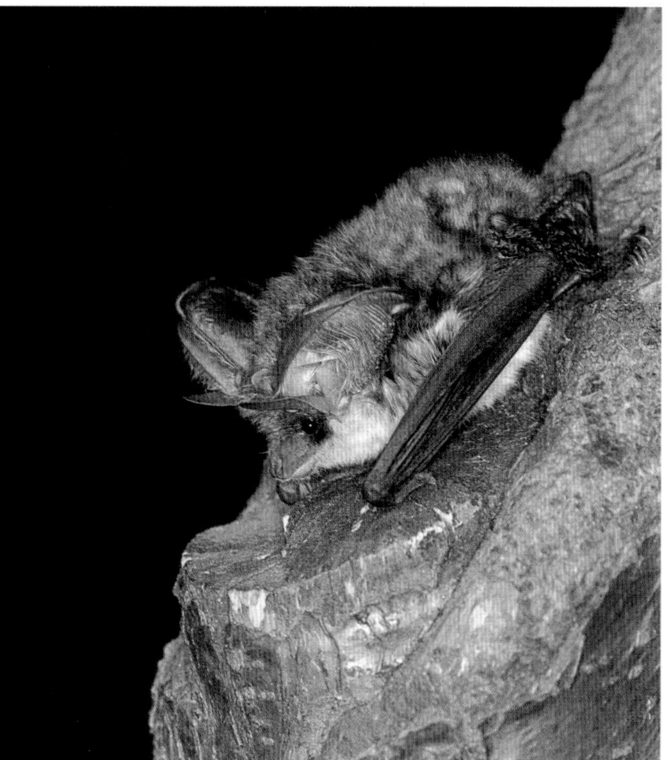

A bat's wing is very much like a re-shaped human hand. The small thumb is free and has a claw, which is needed for climbing. Together with the hind legs and the tail, the remaining four middle-hand and finger bones—which are greatly lengthened—stretch out the flight membrane.

Tree-Dweller

With its narrow wings, the great noctule bat is a swift flyer, reaching speeds of more than 31 m.p.h. (50 km/h). This furry bat takes to the air just before sundown. It hunts mainly flying insects that live in treetops along rivers and lakes. If it gets thirsty, it can fly low and take a sip from the water's surface!

Old and vacated woodpecker holes are common sleeping places for the great noctule bat. Here, during the summer, the female rears her young. In the fall, noctule bats sometimes roam hundreds of miles away to reach their winter sleeping quarters. These hibernation homes can be anything from tree hollows, to boxes, to rock crevices, to spaces behind wall boards.

Above left: *Often, the actual builders of the noctule bat's home are woodpeckers.*

Above right: *Before a noctule bat slips into a new tree hollow, it sniffs the entrance carefully. This is to make sure it's not already occupied! The male will defend its home very forcefully during mating time in the fall, and will furiously chase away any rival that comes near.*

Protecting Bats

It is sad, but many bats around the world are severely endangered today. These shy, harmless insect hunters rely on a rich landscape to survive. They need to hunt insects that dwell in individual trees, hedges and shrubs, forests, river plains, and pastures. Such wild and undisturbed natural habitats must be preserved in order for them to survive.

Nocturnal animals are not easy to observe. This is especially true for bats. Nonetheless, with ultrasound detectors, bat researchers have already been able to learn much about these creatures. With these devices, scientists are able to hear ultrasonic sounds and can therefore track bats and study their hunting and feeding practices. Often, researchers can even determine the species of bat by its echolocation sounds.

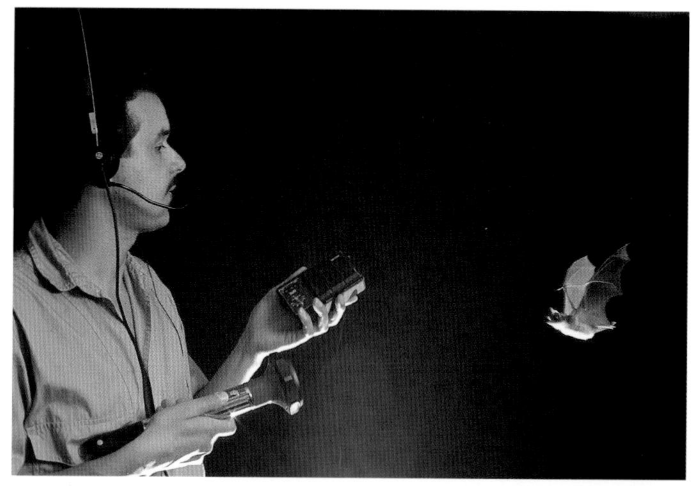

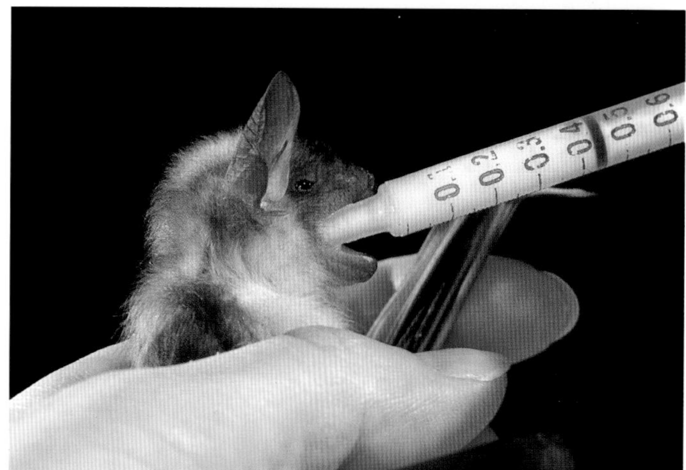

Left: *Preserving bat habitats is essential to preserving bat species.*

Above top: *A researcher uses an ultrasound detector to learn more about echolocation.*

Above bottom: *A baby bat is cared for in a research laboratory.*

Above: *A frosted bat rests on the bark of a tree. Its frosted fur blends with the color of the bark. This "camouflaging" helps to protect bats from their predators.*

The more we study bats, and learn about their amazing abilities, the more we respect and admire them. And the more we understand how bats live, the better we can work to protect them. With bat populations declining in many parts of the world, humans must take responsibility for helping these creatures to survive. Without our help, the world is in great danger of losing some of nature's most mysterious and remarkable animals.

For More Information

Ackerman, Diane. *Bats: Shadows in the Night*. New York: Crown Publishing Group, 1997.

Arnold, Caroline. *Bat*. New York: William Morrow & Co., 1996.

Glaser, Linda. *Beautiful Bats*. Brookfield, CT: Millbrook Press, 1997.

Gray, Susan Heinrichs. *Bats*. Danbury, CT: Children's Press, 1997.

Greenaway, Frank. *Amazing Bats*. New York: Knopf, 1991.

Johnson, Sylvia A. *Bats*. Minneapolis, MN: Lerner Publications Company, 1989.

L'Hommedieu, John. *Bats*. New York: Childs Play International, 1995.

Penny, Malcolm. *How Bats 'See' in the Dark*. New York: Marshall Cavendish, 1997.

Perry, Phyllis Jean. *The Amazing Upside-Downers*. Danbury, CT: Franklin Watts, 1998.

Stuart, Dee. *Bats: Mysterious Flyers of the Night*. Minneapolis, MN: Carolrhoda Books, 1994.

Index

Boldface type indicates photos

Photo Credits

Page 5: ©Hans Pfletschinger/Peter Arnold, Inc.; pages 36–37: ©Blackbirch Press, Inc.